JOSH WEIDMANN

RAISING
SCREEN TIME
KIDS

Biblical Principles for Parenting
in a Device Saturated World

For My Newest Little Buddy, Patten.

As I write this dedication, you are sitting still next to me, with your little head and whole-body weight leaning against my chest. You watch the cursor flicker and the words form. You keep making sweet little cooing sounds filled with fascination.

Screens will forever be a part of your life.

I pray you use them to consume content that nourishes your soul.
I pray you will avoid the pitfalls of luring sin that technology can bring.
I pray you find a way to make the Gospel of Jesus Christ known through devices.

I started this book right before you came, continued writing it around your birth, delayed it while you were in the ICU, and finished as you turned three months old. Little buddy, this book came into existence as you came into my life. I pray the principles in here will be lived out in you all the way through adulthood.

Live for Christ, Patten. There is nothing else worth living for.

I love you, buddy.

CONTENTS

Why Kids Crave Screens. 5
Core Principle #1 Even though screens are a regular part of our everyday lives, they don't have to control us.

The Good, The Bad, and The Ugly 13
Core Principle #2 Screen time, in and of itself, is rarely the problem. How we see God, ourselves, and other people as a result of our screen time often is the problem.

Nothing Replaces Personal Connection 23
Core Principle #3 Face-to-face time with your children will help you reach their hearts, not just fill their minds.

Raising Responsible Digital Citizens 31
Core Principle #4 Being responsible with screens is a discipleship opportunity, not a parenting obstacle.

Leading by Example 39
Core Principle #5 How your kids see you use your screens is how they will expect to use their screens in the future.

Setting Healthy Boundaries for Screens 49
Core Principle #6 A primary responsibility of parents in this digital age is to help their children develop healthy boundaries with screens.

Helping Your Child Develop Healthy Screen Habits . . . 61
Core Principle #7 If you teach your kids to use their screens in moderation when they are young, it's likely they will carry this life skill into adulthood.

The Chief End of Raising Screen Time-Savvy Kids 71

Core Principles #8 Every moment we use a screen is an opportunity to bring glory to God.

What Should You Do If Your Child Has an Addiction to Screens and Refuses Help? 79

Core Principle #9 Screen addiction is a serious, clinically diagnosable condition that can have devastating effects if not addressed early, intentionally, and biblically.

The Only Two Rules You Need 91

Core Principle #10 Screens, like money or time, are amoral in nature. It's how we use those devices to fulfill the greatest commandment of Christ that matters most.

CORE PRINCIPLE #1

EVEN THOUGH
SCREENS ARE A
REGULAR PART OF
OUR EVERYDAY
LIVES, THEY
DON'T HAVE TO
CONTROL US.

CHAPTER 1

WHY KIDS CRAVE SCREENS

START WITH SCRIPTURE

"Be sober-minded; be watchful. Your adversary the devil prowls around like a roaring lion, seeking someone to devour." – 1 Peter 5:8

CORE PRINCIPLE #1

Even though screens are a regular part of our everyday lives, they don't have to control us.

The average American adult spends seven hours and fifty minutes a day consuming content on a screen.[1] Let that sink in for a moment: *nearly one-third of your twenty-four-hour day is spent looking at a device.* One report noted an increase of one hour per day across devices year-over-year, and analysts anticipate daily screen time

....

1   Ethan Cramer-Flood, "US Time Spent with Media 2021 Update," eMarketer, Feb. 4, 2021, https://www.emarketer.com/content/us-time-spent-with-media-2021-update, accessed on Nov. 15, 2021

will only increase in the future. Technology and screens are a significant part of day-to-day life in this world, for adults and kids alike around the world. Adults use them for work, communication, chores, and entertainment. We even look at restaurant menus on our mobile devices! In the same way, children use technology to do homework, connect with friends, learn, and play.

It's virtually impossible to get away from screens. As technology keeps advancing, screens will continue to play a vital role in our lives. Parents must be aware of the pros and cons before considering how screen time affects their children's behaviors, development, and family dynamics. The questions we set out to answer in this book are: *How can you build healthy relationships with technology? and How can you help your children do the same?*

We can live in a screen-saturated world while still bringing glory to God by thinking about technology from a biblical perspective. Our kids are malleable—and if you're not careful, they will be much more influenced by what their screens say than what you say. As stewards of our children's faith and discipleship, we can't afford to cede that battleground.

Why Are Children So Obsessed with Technology?

What is your child doing right now? He or she is likely glued to a screen, be it a computer, TV, or mobile device, or is sitting somewhere close to a screen, even if it isn't on. Kids are always on the go and never content with being bored for even five minutes. All of my six kids (yes, I know, six kids is a lot!) seem to wake up like addicts. They start looking for screen time the moment their eyes open.

Don't we do the same thing as adults? As soon as our alarms go off—alarms set on our phones, ironically—we roll over, hit "Stop" or "Snooze" (guilty), and immediately scroll through our notifications. Again, I'm just as guilty as the next person of letting my heart rush toward a screen before I thank God that I woke up. Our kids are wired the same way.

All of my kids knew how to unlock (or at least try) my iPhone by their first birthday. By the age of two, children are already experts at using screens. They recognize the icons of their favorite apps and know how to push the right buttons on the TV remote before they can even speak a complete sentence. By the time they are old enough to go to school, they've been watching their favorite cartoons for years and have "helped" Mom and Dad check their emails or social media feeds many times. They smile for photos or laugh at Grandma and Grandpa while FaceTiming with them. They sing and dance along with cartoon characters. Their little brains are like sponges, ready to soak up any information. In many ways, screens have been there all their lives—and they're addictive.

As parents, we worry about our children's lack of physical activity and social skills, but this is only one side of the coin. Kids generally do need less screen time—but more importantly, they need smarter screen time. Technology isn't all bad: it can teach young children valuable life lessons, such as problem-solving and how to use technology responsibly. The Bible often speaks about how we are to have all things in moderation (for example, 1 Corinthians 10:31; Philippians 4:5; and 1 Corinthians 9:25). Screens are not the enemy; our fickle hearts are. What we do with screens and how we consume them deserves great intentionality.

The Dopamine Effect

With our busy lives, it's easier than ever for us to open our phones and put on a game or YouTube video to get a screaming kid to keep quiet. The cell phone has become the modern-day pacifier. Parents use the soothing chemicals produced by the pleasure center of a child's brain so they can finish their conversations, shopping, or work.

While it's easy to believe our kids are the only ones being pacified by a cellphone or device, we must realize that we are being lulled by its numbing effects as well. Think about your relationship with your cellphone and social media. You might not be able to put it down, and there might be times when social media can feel a little addictive—especially when you check your phone every ten minutes to see if you've received a notification.

Notifications, likes, and comments make us feel "happy" because our brains release a chemical called dopamine. It's the body's reward system—your God-given high-five. Dopamine teases our "feel-good" responses and plays a crucial role in motivation, happiness, forming new habits, and our sense of reward after achieving a goal or completing a task. However, that feeling can be addictive and lead to compulsive behavior. Even those of us who can remember life before the internet, smartphones, and on-demand television programming struggle to regulate our screen time. Imagine being a child who's lived with screens his entire life.

Science has proven that our screens provide the same adrenal dopamine hit in our bodies that come with any other pleasant experience—whether that's eating a piece of chocolate cake or taking a snort of cocaine. This feeling can create a "dopamine loop" in our behavior—a habitual chain of activities that we engage in to force our neurotransmitters to fire off a shot of dopamine. This short-term feedback loop creates a dependency on our devices that can feel impossible to break. Just as a cocaine addict must go through withdrawals when attempting to detoxify himself, so our kids can find themselves having to break a craving that seems stronger than their willpower to withstand it.

A dopamine loop of screen time looks something like this:

- Access to a screen triggers feelings of pleasure.
- Performing an action on the screen (such as pushing "play" or hearing introductory music) provides the initial "hit."
- The ongoing activity on the screen releases feelings of reward, and the longer it lasts the harder it can be to stop it.
- When the activity ceases, the dopamine decreases or is cut off—but the craving remains or will return.
- The cycle begins again.

Lauren Vinopal, a health journalist in New York City, explains it this way:

Dopamine is a neurotransmitter that works by traveling between different synapses and neurons in different parts of the brain that control when and how people eat, sleep, move, learn, and maintain attention. When people are triggered by some sort of external stimuli, like Paw Patrol or methamphetamine, a rush of dopamine is released through neural pathways to the reward system. This tells a person what they're doing feels good and they should do more of it.[2]

That is all a bit scary, right? Our phones and screens already have changed us, and scientists are working hard to understand the long-term effects they are having on our kids. We do know that pathological cell phone use has led to several new terms specifically related to cell phones, including:

- *Phantom vibrations* – the feeling that your phone is vibrating or ringing when it isn't. Hey, was that your phone? (You just checked your phone, didn't you? I do it, too. That's what phantom vibrations do—they're the silent "chirp" for your attention.)
- *Nomophobia* – the fear of being without your phone.
- *Textaphrenia* – the fear that you won't be able to send or receive texts.

In a later chapter of this book, we will explore the similarities between excessive cell phone use and other behavioral addictions, like compulsive gambling.

Pastor Charles R. Swindoll once said, "Each day of our lives, we make deposits in the memory banks of our children." Like you, I

....

2   Lauren Vinopal, "How Screen Time Creates Kid 'Dopamine Addicts' With Bad Habits," Fatherly, May 3, 2019, https://www.fatherly.com/health-science/screen-time-hurts-kids-dopamine-addiction/ accessed on November 17, 2021.

want my kids to know and remember that I love them more than I loved any device in my life. I want to ensure that the deposits that come from their time on a screen are correct, formative, and God-honoring. In this book, we'll delve into biblical and practical steps you can take to build better, healthier relationships with technology for yourself and your children.

SCREEN TIME, IN AND OF ITSELF, IS RARELY THE PROBLEM. HOW WE SEE GOD, OURSELVES, AND OTHER PEOPLE AS A RESULT OF OUR SCREEN TIME OFTEN IS THE PROBLEM.

CHAPTER 2

THE GOOD, THE BAD, AND THE UGLY

START WITH SCRIPTURE

"My son, do not lose sight of these—keep sound wisdom and discretion, and they will be life for your soul and adornment for your neck." – Proverbs 3:21–22

CORE PRINCIPLE #2

Screen time, in and of itself, is rarely the problem. How we see God, ourselves, and other people as a result of our screen time often is the problem.

I am a morning person. I love to wake up when the house is still quiet and tiptoe downstairs to brew my pour-over coffee. I then proceed to my leather chair with my Bible and stack of books.

My favorite mornings are in the summer when the sun is rising, the birds are chirping, and the family is sleeping in.

Or at least they are supposed to be...

Last summer, I found it extremely difficult to get up before everyone else. I would sneak past the bedrooms and down the creaky stairs to the kitchen to start the water for my coffee. Yet, while I stood there, assuming I had risen before everyone else, I would hear the faint sound of voices—the kind that seemed to be coming through small speakers, slightly muffled, yet conveying some kind of pitchy energy over a crazy stunt or selfie video.

My kids (at least one of them, but sometimes two or three of my six kids) would get up earlier than any kid should in the summer just to grab a cell phone, tablet, or laptop. Like cyberspies, they either would hack through our parental-control passwords or recall them from the one time they looked over our shoulders, and voila they were in! I would find them by following the sound to discover them curled up on the side of the couch, in the basement, or in their closets with the doors closed.

Talk about feeling like I was living with a bunch of addicts! My kids would sacrifice sweet sleep to take a hit before dawn, then slither into small places to feed their craving without getting caught. That's when I decided to get to the bottom of the screen-time addiction. Was this just innocent entertainment, or had they truly become dependent on devices?

What is the right amount of screen time a kid should have?

Researchers at the National Institutes of Health report that nearly half of all children ages eight and under have their own tablet.[1] The percentage only grows for those between ages twelve and fifteen, and nearly everyone age sixteen or older owns their own device. That is millions of personal devices in the hands of our kids! Don't get me wrong, the fact that the child has a device is not the problem (though it could add to it); it is what that child does with the device that we are focusing on.

A child spends an average of 2.25 hours a day on digital screens, according to Common Sense Media.[2] Does this sound like a lot to you? Just think about it—add up the time your child has been on a screen of any kind just today. Is it around two hours?

During a recent wellness check, our pediatrician reminded our elementary-aged children to eat their fruits and vegetables, make sure to get in some good protein, drink their milk, and limit their screen time to two hours per day.

It was as if screen consumption has now been added to the classic "food pyramid."[3] My kids were reminded that a healthy diet did not contain too much sugar—or screens. The doctor explained that the two-hour benchmark includes all the time they spend

....

1 "What Does Too Much Screen Time do to Children's Brains," Health Matters, New York Presbyterian Hospital, https://healthmatters.nyp.org/what-does-too-much-screen-time-do-to-childrens-brains/.

2 "Landmark Report: U.S. Teens Use an Average of Nine Hours of Media Per Day, Tweens Use Six Hours," Common Sense Media, Nov. 3, 2015, https://www.commonsensemedia.org/about-us/news/press-releases/landmark-report-us-teens-use-an-average-of-nine-hours-of-media-per-day-tweens-use-six-hours accessed on Nov. 15, 2021.

3 "Food Pyramid (nutrition)," Wikipedia, https://en.wikipedia.org/wiki/Food_pyramid_(nutrition).

on screens at school. I shudder to think that most of our kids are consuming more than two hours per day of screen time, *especially* if that number includes school. Are we feeding their addiction—even creating it—and then expecting these small people to have self-control?

While quantity is a concern, and something we will address later in this book, the content they are consuming is our first focus.

Screens and the content they deliver don't always make the best company for children—or for adults, for that matter. Yet, on the other hand, there is a wealth of content that can enrich our lives, even if that means it simply brings a smile to our faces on a rainy day. The ancient Greeks had a saying that still resonates with people today: *Moderation in all things.* We can certainly see how this adage applies to screen time. To truly understand the depths of the effect of screens on our minds, emotions, and behavior, let's look at the good, the bad, and the ugly of screen time.

The Good

Screen time can have many positive benefits for children. Students project things, interact with things, listen to things, watch things, and write things—all on screens. When a child in today's generation enters school and later, the workforce, he or she will encounter countless forms of technology. The bright spots in screen time for kids are:

- **Connectivity.** They can connect with parents, teachers, relatives, and friends over a device that used to cost a lot of money. Now, with the press of a button, they can connect with anyone, anywhere, instantly.

- **Technical prowess.** Their navigation skills and overall tech know-how increase as they work on screens. This is a vital skill to make it in our ever-advancing world.
- **Exposure.** Screens allow them to see things without traveling or leaving the comfort of home.
- **Learning.** A wealth of educational content is delivered to screens, but parents must carefully curate what our kids are accessing to make sure it's good content, not negative content. They can learn good or bad things with equal ease.
- **Tracking.** Apps can track healthy behaviors. For instance, kids can track their reading minutes, number of steps taken per day, or read daily inspirational messages that support their faith and spirituality.
- **Reasoning.** Parents have to remember that kids aren't able to critically assess different types of screen content. Parents must use proper guidelines or safeguards to help them learn how to make wise decisions.

The Bad

Screens are not sinful in and of themselves. What we do with them can be. Job 4:8 says, "According to what I have seen, those who plow iniquity and those who sow trouble harvest it."

Although there are many positive aspects of screen time that parents can encourage children to enjoy, there is certainly a negative side to it. We can "sow iniquity" that will reap a lifetime of "trouble" if we are not careful with our devices. There is a seemingly endless parade of inane programming and other content that's about as mentally nourishing as a pile of sawdust—not to mention that some of it is pornographic and that all kinds of predators use technology to reach out directly to your kids. At best, content like this is like consuming empty calories; at worst, it's like drinking poison. (More on this in the next section.)

Fundamentally, too much screen time is unhealthy for children of any age. According to the U.S. Library of Medicine,[4] too much screen time can lead to disrupted sleep patterns, increase the risk of attention-deficit disorders, contribute to mood disturbances like irritability and anxiety, and raise the risk of obesity.

If you were born in the 1980s or before, you may remember that classic commercial that said, "This is your brain on drugs." The public service announcement sponsored by the federal government[5] showed a man standing in an apartment with an egg and a frying pan. He holds up an egg and says, "This is your brain," before motioning to the frying pan and adding, "This is drugs." He then cracks open the egg, fries the contents, and says, "This is your brain on drugs."

Finally, he looks up at the camera and asks, "Any questions?"

While the analogy effectively explained narcotics, it could paint a vivid picture of our brains on screens. Too much time on a device

....

4   Caitlyn Fuller, Eric Lehman, Steven Hicks, and Marsha B. Novick, MD,"Bedtime Use of Technology and Associated Sleep Problems in Children," Global Pediatric Health, Oct. 27, 2017, https://www.ncbi.nlm.nih.gov/pmc/articles/PMC5669315/ accessed on Nov. 15, 2021.
5   Wikipedia, "This is your brain on drugs" https://en.wikipedia.org/wiki/This_Is_Your_Brain_on_Drugs

can slow or change a child's brain as it develops—which doesn't stop until he reaches the age of twenty-one.

A lot of content available to children may not be outright horrible; it might even be socially acceptable, but simply not in line with your values as a follower of Jesus. Again, it's crucial for parents to curate what their kids watch. This is especially important when they are younger, because your efforts to help them create healthy habits may become more difficult once they hit their teen years.

We want our kids to feel happy and to enjoy their lives, especially after they work their brains all day in school. However, there are so many other forms of entertainment besides fluffy TV shows that offer no substance. Encourage children to try some of these activities instead of gluing their eyes to another screen:

- Play with the dog (or other pets)
- Read
- Draw
- Play at the park
- Ride a bike
- Put a puzzle together
- Do a craft
- Build a backyard fort

For example, I am willing to spend just about any amount of money on my kids at Hobby Lobby because that means they are doing something creative with their hands, not a screen—anything from building model cars to sculpting to weaving a rug.

The Ugly

The internet, for all its good, does certainly brim with mature content that offers nothing positive to children or *adults*. Moreover, it's amazingly easy for even our youngest kids to access it. Just consider: you hand your phone to one of your younger children to keep him occupied with TikTok videos of puppies while you're trying to have a conversation with another parent at a soccer game—and then suddenly find he's eyeballing videos of adults kissing, vaping, twerking, and God only knows what else. It's that easy—and all just a tap away.

It only gets easier for kids to access questionable or prurient content online as they get older because they often understand how to navigate devices better than their parents do. The average age of first exposure to pornography is now eight years old.[6] As parents, we can't afford to simply shrug our shoulders and give up so easily. To not fight for your child's innocence is to abdicate your God-given responsibility as a parent. You simply cannot be passive about your children's screen time. You must take an active role in protecting your kids from bad actors or content that's simply too mature for young eyes. This isn't just your kid's mind at stake; it's his future marriage, her perspective on love and relationships, and most importantly, what they believe is permissible and not sinful in the eyes of our Creator God.

There are other "Ugly" sides to the screen world, such as cyberbullying, online predators, and violent games. Our kids are facing

....

6 Jim Daly and Paul Asay, *When Parenting Isn't Perfect*, (Grand Rapids, MI: Zondervan, 2017).

the painful challenge of bullying extending well past the school-yard and into their homes through their devices. Online predators no longer just lurk in creepy-looking vans around parks. With the anonymity that screens can offer, it is impossible to know who is on the other side of a device. Too much unsupervised access and unlimited use can leave our children vulnerable to people who have evil and perverse intentions.

Of course, their peers will pressure them to play the latest video games, which that often feature violence in one form or another. I Corinthians 15:33 says, "Do not be misled. Bad company corrupts good character." When we think that the screen isn't affecting our kids, we must think again.

There are violence- and sex-free videos and online games that promote learning, but there is a strong likelihood these are not the most popular ones your child and his or her friends are longing for. Take heart. This is an opportunity to help your kids develop character by engaging with the right things and avoiding those trappings that detract from their spiritual beliefs, practices, and values.

Yes, there are good, bad, and ugly aspects of screen time. However, being a fully engaged, Gospel-centered parent who actively disciples your child is the best way to help him grow in his faith and future as a follower of Jesus. Stay strong, and stay present.

CORE PRINCIPLE #3

FACE-TO-FACE TIME WITH YOUR CHILDREN WILL HELP YOU REACH THEIR HEARTS, NOT JUST FILL THEIR MINDS.

CHAPTER 3

NOTHING REPLACES PERSONAL CONNECTION

START WITH SCRIPTURE

"And let us not grow weary of doing good, for in due season we will reap, if we do not give up." — Galatians 6:9

CORE PRINCIPLE #3

Face-to-face time with your children will help you reach their hearts, not just fill their minds.

Do you know parents who love the "things" of being a kid? (Or maybe you are one.) They love Disney every bit as much as their kids do. They collect Star Wars action figures. They plan flag football plays. They happily spend the greater part of an evening building Legos skyscrapers or arranging Barbie's wardrobe. If you don't enjoy these things with your child, it doesn't mean you're lacking as a parent, but seeing you playing with the things they love could mean the world to your children.

For our kids to find a healthy balance with technology, they need to connect with humans. What human should be more important for your child to connect with every day than you? Some days, it's hard to ignore our stresses, work headaches, and problems. It's easy to turn on the television or hand your kids a device so you can catch a break. I get that—I'm just as guilty of that as anyone else, but letting that happen too often can sabotage your goal to limit screen time (for yourself as well as your kids). Even more, it can consistently rob you of an amazing opportunity to connect with your child.

When someone asks me, "How would you describe parenting— especially with six kids at home?" I usually say, "FAST." The time with your kids goes so *fast*. There's a saying that the days are long but the years are short. You only have these kids in your care for a short period of time and then *poof*! It's gone. If you've hit the adolescent years, you already know that you lose your welcomed impact and oversight in their lives far before they leave your home.

Connecting with Your Young Children

It's not fancy vacations or elaborate birthday gifts that build your kids' characters—it's you engaging with them. Young kids have so many basic needs. With all of your schedule demands, work responsibilities, and needs that come with taking care of your home, it can be hard to fit in quality time. It's too easy to put off reading together because you need to fold a basket of laundry or write one last email for the day—but what's more important?

You need to prioritize time to connect with your children—time when you give them your undivided attention. These are bonding moments, teaching moments. You can use this time to pray together, talk about Jesus in a way they understand, read storybooks, or even play with Legos while chatting about their day. You can engage in activities that spark meaningful moments with your children. You have it within you to show your kids activities that are just as enjoyable as any screen.

Connecting with Older Children and Teens

It's natural for older children and teens to desire more independence as they grow. If they're already used to balancing technology with other activities like biking, swimming, dancing, or playing a sport, they may not need you to guide their screen time so much because they've already developed healthy habits. However, they still need to connect with you and others in meaningful ways.

Older children, especially teens, go through so many changes. It's important for you to be tuned into their developmental needs as they occur. Think about ways you can spend quality time with your older children that will strengthen your bond, your ability to communicate well, and your enjoyment of one another. Here are a few ideas to inspire you:

- Take an art class together
- Listen to an audiobook together

- Plan a retreat or attend a church retreat together
- Take the family dog to obedience classes and train together
- Get into a walking routine together
- Volunteer together

None of these activities involves a screen, so you can help your children reduce their screen time while connecting over something truly enjoyable. As your children get older, you may be amazed how short both the days and the years become before they're off to college and out in the real world.

In my book, *Dad, If You Only Knew*, I explain the longing that teenagers have to be heard. My mom and dad were exceptional at listening to me, and admittedly, I fail to meet their standard with my own kids. My mom would take us out to dinner on the other side of town on purpose so we would have the whole car ride to talk. My dad would take us camping to keep us away from the daily distractions so we could talk on a hike or around the campfire. I knew my parents were willing to listen because they would say things like:

- Mom: You are welcome at my counter any day. Come sit and talk to me while I make dinner. You decide the topic.
- Dad: I placed that chair in my home office for you. Anytime you want to talk about something, come sit in it, and I'll stop what I am doing so we can chat. No agenda. No time limit.

To this day, I can say that my mom and dad drop their devices, turn off their distractions, and give me their undivided attention when I want to talk. As their child, I can only hope to provide them the same respect and, in turn, do the same for my kids.

Connect with Their Friends

By being involved with your older kids, you'll also have an opportunity to get to know their friends. Even if it was more than a few years ago, at one time, you were a teen. You understand what peer pressure is, whether you succumbed to it at some point or not. You also had friends who chose negative paths. As you involve yourself in your children's day-to-day lives, be involved as you can with their friends so you can get to know them and, hopefully, model good behavior for them. Not all kids will have parents who are willing to tune in closely. You may find that your son's or daughter's friends enjoy spending time at your home, and that's a positive sign.

Just remember that your kids will never stop needing your emotional support. As they grow, they'll require less and less "physical" support, but they'll need your guidance and the benefit of your experience. By connecting with them routinely, you'll find it easier to connect with them when they're going through rough patches. You want them to rely on you and benefit from your example of turning to God when you're facing a crisis. You don't want them to turn to a screen or to friends who may not have the right answers or guidance for them before they turn to you.

Wisdom Is Caught, Not Taught

The entire book of Proverbs is a model of a parent imparting wisdom to his child. While there is a teaching element to Proverbs, this crown jewel of biblical advice is written in as relational instruction, sharing the patterns of godly living with the next generation. More than fifty times, the word "son" is used; in addition, many other terms like "my child" (Proverbs 20:11, 22:6, 22:15, 23:13, and 29:15), which can also be translated as "babe," "boy," "child," "damsel," "lad," "servant," or "young man." If we are going to help our children make wise decisions, we must have enough of a relationship with them to be able to speak to their hearts' affections as well as their minds.

I want nothing more for my kids than to walk in Christlikeness as they navigate life. If I am going to help them overcome the temptations and pains of this world, I must cultivate the kind of relationship with them that will allow me to share God's wisdom. If we are a screen time-saturated household, I likely will not be able to share with them all that God has taught me through life experience, or what His Word has to say for the situations each of us face. My greatest legacy will be to teach my children to fear the Lord, but this will only happen if I peel their eyes (and mine!) off the screen.

> *"The fear of the Lord is the beginning of knowledge; fools despise wisdom and instruction. Hear, My son, your father's instruction, and do not forsake your mother's teaching; indeed, they are a graceful wreath to your head, and ornaments about your neck."*
> *– Proverbs 1:7–9*

CORE PRINCIPLE #4

BEING RESPONSIBLE WITH SCREENS IS A DISCIPLESHIP OPPORTUNITY, NOT A PARENTING OBSTACLE.

CHAPTER 4

RAISING RESPONSIBLE DIGITAL CITIZENS

START WITH SCRIPTURE

"Train up a child in the way he should go; even when he is old, he will not depart from it." – Proverbs 22:6

CORE PRINCIPLE #4

Being responsible with screens is a discipleship opportunity, not a parenting obstacle.

As parents, we want to raise our children "right," and that desire is influenced by what we believe to be true about God, Jesus, the Bible, and other crucial parts of our convictions. We want our children to be good people, make great decisions, be safe, and embody the same principles and values we have as followers of Jesus.

But raising kids in the digital age adds a new dimension to our parenting. We need to raise digitally responsible citizens who understand the good and bad aspects of technology. That responsibility starts with teaching them how to make wise choices with technology now so they can carry those excellent and godly habits into adulthood.

Be Mindful of Age

As parents, we know our kids' different ages require different digital guidelines. Being a good digital citizen at age seven means turning off the game console the first time Dad or Mom asks. Being a good digital citizen as a teen means knowing how to interact with others through whichever social media platform they choose. Being a good digital citizen at any age means not sharing personal information online with strangers or making plans to meet someone in person without your knowledge.

You can take several vital steps to help your child be more God-honoring in a world saturated with devices. As you read through this list, think about modifying these expectations to match your child's current age.

Be Present and Engaged

When your children are young, you can establish a routine of spending screen time together. This allows you to encourage good screen behavior right from the beginning. As your children age and become more independent, you will still need to be mindful about the sites they visit, what they watch, who they connect with, and which games they play. My wife, Molly, and I have done our best to ensure that our kids are right next to us when they are using a screen. We can see what they are watching, clicking on, and consuming. I make regular use of the "Guided Access" feature on my iPhone when I hand it to my young children. This locks the phone into a single app and gives me control over which features my child can access. (You can find this through the "accessibility" settings and even set a shortcut to quickly lock the phone on one app. Be sure to check it out!)

Support Positive Choices

It is important to voice your approval when your kids are displaying traits of positive digital citizenship. For instance, congratulate them on making the right choice to tell you when a friend or school acquaintance is being targeted by a cyberbully. Let them know you're aware of how they're sticking to your family's screen rules. Children often want to know you're aware of their good behavior and aren't merely pointing out their missteps. I am quick to praise my kids for making a wise digital decision. I let them know if they watched a show or listened to something that I fully approve of.

Talk About Personal Safety and Digital Safety

Kids need to be aware that the internet is very much like a large meeting place. I've compared it to a crowded airport or sports arena when explaining this to my kids. There are real people connected to the internet from all over the world. They need to know they are not necessarily safe simply because they're in their own home and not physically face-to-face with a stranger. Teach kids never to give out their personal information, such as their last name, school, or address. They should also avoid clicking on potentially nefarious downloads or opening risky emails that could open up their computer to malware. Our church's counseling ministry has seen its fair share of kids brought in after becoming addicted to connecting online with people who have sinister motives. These strangers have been able to get network passwords, computer passwords, and even their parents' credit card information out of these kids. There are thieves and predators out there, and we must make sure that our children are safe and learn how to make wise choices.

Have a Plan for Better Tech Etiquette

As parents, I hope you frequently discuss how to be a good follower of Jesus with your children. Remind them that God's Word teaches us how to interact with others, including online; that means exercising kindness and good manners when engaging with their friends through a screen. They should not participate in cyberbullying or share in spreading rumors or harmful digital content about another person. I have heard horror stories of preteens and teens sharing pictures and rumors about others through text messages or social media that take over the whole school. The targeted teen is mortified and embarrassed at best— and suicidal at worst. The virtual world is still part of the natural world, and God sees and knows there are real humans on the other side of online experiences.

Explain the Consequences of Online Actions

Actions have both good and bad consequences, and that applies to the digital realm as well. When teens share a risqué photo of themselves online, they must be aware that it could wind up traveling far and wide. Such images can affect their reputations and threaten their safety. Moreover, these behaviors could also impact future college entrance and employment opportunities. Even apps that claim the image is gone or disappears after a period are not safe. The digital world has a *long memory* and things can surface years later.

I have personally felt the sting of something I said online being used against me. The digital world is like an ocean: we can play in it and ride the waves, but we must always be aware of the undertow and what lies beneath. Does your child understand that the internet is unforgiving in this way? It is important that we explain these realities to our children without causing undue fear.

You Can Do It!

Raising kids in a screen-saturated world is not all negative. I have outlined some of the hazards, but we must not throw out the baby with the bathwater. There are opportunities for Gospel impact that come with being good digital citizens. If we use technology correctly, we can bring the light of Christ to the world in ways that previous generations could only dream of doing. Examples would be:

- Spreading awareness of the plight of those who are being mistreated

- Learning about others' experiences or stories
- Encouraging others with God's Word or by sharing what He is doing in our life
- Connecting with other Christians around the world
- Using our devices to do the work of evangelism and encouragement
- Sharing about a cause or opportunity to help others

In the same way we train our kids to be positive influences in our culture—by helping others in need, not littering, respecting property, and using manners—we also can teach them how to use technology to give back to the world around them.

Does raising smart digital citizens seem overwhelming? There's a lot to it—it involves keeping up with privacy controls and checking every device's browsing history so you know where your kids have been and what they've been viewing online. You'll often hear people remark on how hard it is to raise kids these days. But the truth is, it's always been hard. It was hard for Israelite parents during their captivity in Egypt. Parenting was hard during times of plague, famine, wars, the Industrial Age, and the Sexual Revolution. Realistically, you understand it will be difficult in the future as well. This is where we lean into the words our Savior Jesus spoke to His disciples:

> *"In this world, you will have trouble. But take heart! I have over-come the world." – John 16:33*

Remember that you are not alone as you struggle to raise your children. Lean on your faith, on prayer, on your church community and pastor, and on your loved ones who share your faith. Jesus gives you the strength to set goals for raising your children, as well as the ability to achieve those goals. By focusing on raising digitally wise children, you can instill important values in them that they'll carry well into adulthood.

Our greatest calling as parents isn't necessarily to raise great kids—it's to raise great adults. The difference is in how we empower our kids to take responsibility for the screens we allow into their lives.

Your kids will make mistakes, just like you have (and do), but God has entrusted you with their discipleship and care. Even in your lowest moments of feeling inadequate, there is a God in Heaven who still says, "I made you for this moment. You're *their* parent for a reason."

As much as we want to raise great digital citizens, our ultimate citizenship is in Heaven with our Creator God and Savior Jesus Christ. How we live, both on and off our screens, says more about what we value in light of eternity. Discipleship starts with our hearts, and how we model responsible digital ownership of our devices merely reflects those values.

CORE PRINCIPLE #5

HOW YOUR KIDS SEE YOU USE YOUR SCREENS IS HOW THEY WILL EXPECT TO USE THEIR SCREENS IN THE FUTURE.

CHAPTER 5

LEADING BY EXAMPLE

START WITH SCRIPTURE

"If we live by the Spirit, let us also keep in step with the Spirit." – Galatians 5:25

CORE PRINCIPLE #5

How your kids see you use your screens is how they will expect to use their screens in the future.

There is an old adage that says, "More is caught than taught." Our actions are the most impactful teachers for our children. Without a doubt, whether our behavior is right or wrong, our kids see, learn, and all too often mimic what we do.. If we use certain words, they will too. If we eat healthy food, they will too. And if we struggle with some kind of addiction—including to our screens—studies show that they will, too. Our actions matter!

If we tell our children that too much screen time is bad, but remain glued to our devices throughout the day, our actions convey the truth—and kids will believe what they see us doing far more than they believe what they hear us saying. It takes considerable self-discipline to model the right behavior all the time, but if we're mindful, we can model the actions we want our children to embrace. That doesn't mean we can't access our screens or enjoy more grown-up content, but we need to be mindful when we do.

Regretfully, I am really good at having entire conversations with my family without ever looking up from the screen. It is scary to think that young children are more accustomed to seeing the logo on the back of our cell phones than they are to seeing our faces. I don't want mine to remember their dad more from an Apple logo than a compassionate smile or meaningful eye contact. Think of how the Lord deals with us. He said, "I will instruct you and teach you in the way you should go; I will counsel you with My loving eye on you" (Psalm 32:8). Though He has the whole world to watch over, He doesn't take His loving eyes off of us.

Before we go much deeper into talking about raising screen-time kids, let's talk about what it means to be a responsible screen-time adult. Here are a few pointers for us as parents:

Evaluate Your Screen Time

Take time to reflect on how you use technology and what types of content you watch. Is it educational? Is it spiritually support-ive? Does it inspire you to do well, to improve? How much fluff versus substantial content do you consume each day throughout the week? How many "empty entertainment calories" are you devouring?

Recently, I was thinking about how I scroll 15-second videos on a social media site. I told my wife, "I think when I look at all these short videos, it is like sitting and eating a bag of Cheetos. It feels good at the moment, it is really hard to stop, and I usually regret it later."

As an adult, you are also vulnerable to the negative aspects of too much screen time. An abuse of it can interfere with sleep patterns and lead to depression, anxiety, and unclear thinking. Moreover, what value are you receiving from this visual content? What are the Kardashians, *Tiger King*, *The Bachelor*, or various other "entertaining" shows doing to promote life-long learning or improve your spiritual well-being? Is peering over the fence into your friend's yard of greener grass helping your soul? How can you reduce your intake of meaningless shows and introduce more enlightening content into your screen-time routine?

In his book, *12 Ways Your Phone is Changing You*, Tony Reinke confesses,

> *My phone is a window into the worthless and the worthy, the artificial and the authentic. Some days, I feel as if my phone is a digital vampire, sucking away my time and my life. Other days, I feel like a cybernetic centaur—part human, part digital—as my phone and I blend seamlessly into a complex tandem of rhythms and routines.*

Many adults like playing videos, surfing social networks, and texting their friends, just as kids do. If you play your favorite video game for four hours on Saturday, guess who'll want to play theirs, too? It's not easy to model good behavior all the time, but your children are well worth the effort. As you take inventory of your tech time, be sure you include all the time you spend gaming, texting, or interacting on social media. If your kids witness you constantly checking your screen, they'll likely pick up this habit—and without the mature discretion or moderation that we usually have as adults.

Small Improvements Lead to Big Changes

After evaluating your screen time, you should set goals for improving your own behavior. If you want your children to watch more educational programming, you have to watch more educational programming. If you want your kids to limit their video gameplay, you have to limit yours.

To accomplish this, you'll want to set parameters for your own screen time use just as you do for your kids. For example, don't set your phone on the table during dinner. Don't watch television shows that are inappropriate for your kids. Don't spend the entire evening scrolling through social media. Instead, let your children see you perform other activities such as:

- Reading
- Meal planning
- Exercising
- Meditating on Scripture
- Gardening
- Crafting or building something with your hands, like

    woodworking, painting, or sculpting

- Attending a Bible study

Use your free time to participate more fully in family life. Enjoy activities with your kids that have nothing to do with screens or technology to ensure they have balance in their lives—and that you have balance in yours.

If needed, you can find apps to help you manage your screen time. If you own an iPhone, there are ScreenTime settings you can access to put time limits and time parameters on certain apps. There are other apps for phone platforms—and even our computers and tablets—that will help you limit screen time by turning the device off or cutting off internet access.

If you find it difficult to do this cold turkey, try to reduce time spent with screens gradually. Try reducing your screen time by 10 or 15 minutes each day until you reach your goal. It may help to enlist a friend to hold you accountable.

If you are truly addicted to an app on your mobile device, you can take a significant step by simply deleting it. If it's work-related, you may want to consider why you're spending so much time on that particular app—and if you *need* to spend that much time on it. The answer is likely, "No, you don't need to use that app that much." Delete it if you can.

At one point, I set a daily reminder to delete an app from my phone. I had well over one hundred of them, and some of them were pure time-wasters. It wasn't so hard to let go of the first ten to fifteen, but then I got into heart-surgery type decisions where I was letting go of apps that required me to check my motives for using them in the first place. I didn't delete all of my apps but pared it down to the essential ones.

If Christ's original audience had the technology we have today, I am pretty sure He would have added, "If your apps are causing you to sin, delete them" to His Sermon on the Mount (see Matthew 5:29). Living in balance and obedience calls for calculated subtractions from your life.

In time, you'll find it easier to limit your use of technology as you fill the time with other activities that enhance your and your family's well-being. But I don't want you to miss something here: healthy technology usage is not all about behavior modification. While we must find limits, we must also be willing to do heart surgery. We must ask questions like:

- Why am I looking at my phone so much?
- In what areas am I finding comfort or pleasure through a screen?
- What do I hope to get out of my online connections?
- What is my motivation in all the scrolling?

The way we answer these questions will point to the desire of our hearts. So often, we are our phones in an effort to fill a God-sized hole for connection, comfort, purpose, or meaning. We are searching for something, but our screens leave us empty-handed—or should I say, empty-hearted. As disciples of Christ, and disciple-makers of our kids, we must be looking for "the why behind the what." Behavior modification says, "Fix the what." But actual change comes when we work on the whys of our life. We must prick our conscience with questions and evaluations that will change our motives and thinking.

Jesus's first sermon in Matthew 4 tells us that actual change begins with something far more profound than adapting behavior. Change was His central theme, and He began by saying, "Repent of your sins and turn to God, for the Kingdom of Heaven is near" (NLT). Repentance is a Holy Spirit-powered ability to change our thinking, motives, and behavior. If you are going to do life differently concerning your screen usage, it must start with *renewing your mind* (Romans 12:2) and depending on the Holy Spirit to change your relationship with technology from the inside out. Romans 8:6 promises, "The mind governed by the flesh is death, but the mind governed by the Spirit is life and peace" (NIV).

True Change Starts at the Top

Think about how your brain guides your body. Very few physical actions are truly involuntary. A vast majority of what you do and say happens because your brain thought of it before your body acted on that impulse. The same is true for your family: as its head, you can help set your family's impulses and responses through what you allow yourself to think, say, and do about your screen time.

If you want to truly change how your family interacts with screens in a healthy, God-honoring way, you need to make the conscious decision to do so. Yes, it may be difficult, but when this life is over and you're standing before our Savior, He won't ask how many levels you unlocked on your favorite game. He won't ask for your follower or post counts. He doesn't care about your likes or comments. He'll ask if you did everything possible to guide your family's hearts toward Christ, to create an incredible life with great memories (with or without screens), to cultivate a Gospel-centered environment in your family dynamics, and to live life fully, with joy and worship.

That doesn't happen by accident. That starts with a heart for discipleship. Discipleship is literally "learning by example." Remember what Paul said in 1 Corinthians 11:1: "Be imitators of me, as I am of Christ." This should be our heart when it comes to helping our kids live out a biblical and healthy perspective on screens; we must model it. Whether in our technology use or anything else, parenting is an opportunity for discipleship. What are we discipling our kids toward—Jesus or the world (tech in this case)? If we are to live in the world and yet not be of it, what does that mean for the example we set in using technology?

Christ is the example of how to disciple: He did it through intentional time spent in conversation with others. He had slow and unhurried interactions to explain what it means to follow Him. Technology disrupts that and takes away those moments of intentionality. Our devices can make us put our kids on hold, interrupt them, or miss out on an opportunity to invest in their souls.

If you're not willing to have a healthier relationship with your screens, then the rest of this book won't matter to you. What will you choose today?

A PRIMARY RESPONSIBILITY OF PARENTS IN THIS DIGITAL AGE IS TO HELP THEIR CHILDREN DEVELOP HEALTHY BOUNDARIES WITH SCREENS.

CHAPTER 6

SETTING HEALTHY BOUNDARIES FOR SCREENS

START WITH SCRIPTURE

"No servant can serve two masters, for either he will hate the one and love the other, or he will be devoted to the one and despise the other." — Luke 16:13

CORE PRINCIPLE #6

A primary responsibility of parents in this digital age is to help their children develop healthy boundaries with screens.

I was already sweating, and we hadn't even left the house. We were on our way to meet some friends, and it was my duty to get all the kids in the car—dressed and with shoes on. (Trying to get six kids under the age of eleven out the door is a herculean feat for anyone.) At some point in the process, I handed my three-year-old, Charlie, my phone just to keep him occupied while I tied shoes, helped get shirts over heads, and packed the small mountain of supplies that seem to come with children. When it was time to get Charlie in the car, I took the phone out of his hand, tucked it in my back pocket, and carried him out the door over my shoulder in a classic fireman's hold.

As I strapped him into the car, Charlie was kicking and screaming. He wasn't upset that we were going somewhere; he was upset I had taken my phone away from him. As I used all my might to buckle him into the car seat, I said, "This feels like I am wrestling a demon." My other kids heard that and later asked about twenty questions about demons—such as if I'd ever actually seen one, if one lived in Charlie, and how I knew what it felt like to wrestle a demon.

If you've ever taken a screen away from a toddler or a teenager, you know it can feel like you're entering a dark spiritual battle. Their eyes change, their tempers emerge, and it becomes a battle of wills. I resolved to stand my ground in that moment; there's nothing I dislike more than fighting with a child who has lost any amount of rational thinking because they've lost access to a screen.

Research shows that suddenly interrupting a child's screen time triggers the same response as a drug user going through "cold-turkey" withdrawal. The hypothalamus—the pleasure center of the brain—will send signals to the rest of the body that say, *"Get that back, at whatever cost!"* Don't believe me? Just go search the internet for videos of kids getting their screens taken away, and you'll see what I mean. Hundreds of parents have posted videos (meaning to be funny, I think?) showing what their kid is like when the gaming unit gets unplugged or the power suddenly goes out. The reactions are downright scary (or should I say, *demonic*)?

The American Academy of Pediatrics recommends no more than one hour of screen time a day for children between the ages of eighteen months and five years. Above age five, the recommendations start to veer all over the place, but the healthiest is approximately one to two hours a day.[1] Not sure what the right amount may be for your kid? Ask your pediatrician, but also use what you know about your own child. For instance, if you know your kid changes past a certain amount of screen time, then try to keep it below that limit. You know your child best.

Now, if your children are anything like mine, you're already laughing at the idea of keeping even an eighteen-month-old away from a screen. The glow of bright, shiny pixels can be enough to grab a toddler's attention in any situation. It seems like parenting beyond the pixels is an uphill battle. Many times, I've allowed our one-year-olds to see a kids' program just so my wife and I could get through an adult conversation. So how do we do better as parents? How can we help our kids, of any age, find a good balance?

....

1   American Academy of Pediatrics, "How Much Should You Limit Kids' Screen Time and Electronics Use?", Very Well Family, March 6, 2021, https://www.verywellfamily.com/american-academy-pediatrics-screen-time-guidelines-1094883

When left to their own devices (pun fully realized), children are unlikely to abide by any limits set for them. They crave structure; they need you to set boundaries with expectations of respecting parameters—and for you to mete out consequences when they do not. Part of raising children is teaching them self-discipline. It does require discipline (tremendous self-discipline from their point of view) to turn off their game console or a YouTube video. What a feat when they're able to show that level of maturity.

Biblical Boundaries

"Boundaries" is a popular buzzword these days, and frankly I think it can be overused or misused. People say that they are "setting boundaries" when they mean they just want to say "no" to a person or relationship in their life. But there is a more biblical approach to boundaries.

Boundaries are not always about protection from outside threats; they can also be about cherishing what we already possess. For example, in Psalm 16:5–7, the psalmist writes, "The boundary lines have fallen for me in pleasant places; surely I have a delightful inheritance." God has given us all goodness in our life, and we draw lines around those things to ensure we are praising God for them and enjoying them to the fullest.

Another example of boundaries is how God gave guidance in the Garden of Eden, not because He wanted to control or coerce Adam and Eve, but because He knew what was best for them. He had wisdom, knowledge, and foresight that they didn't possess. In the same way, we want our kids to know we are protecting them.

We want them to trust our decisions. A huge part of setting biblical boundaries comes down to *relationship*. If we are cultivating a relationship with our kids, they will be more likely to grow in their trust of us. They will believe that Mom and Dad aren't trying to hurt or harm them in some way—they are trying to protect them and do what is best for them.

Boundaries, when set and enforced correctly and biblically, create freedom because we are giving kids space to make the best decision for themselves. Part of this process for parents may be helping our kids choose where to set boundary lines: things like letting them help create the consequences for when they don't follow the rules, letting them choose what they can access from an approved list during their "tech time," etc.

Creating a Screen Contract

You're familiar with the various usage contracts that come with a new phone or tablet. If something breaks, the manufacturer agrees to honor the repair process. As the user, you have a responsibility not to abuse your freedom in using that device. A contract is a legal obligation—an agreement to submit to an authority with clear consequences if you violate the terms. Contracts may be necessary when it comes to guiding our children in making responsible screen-time decisions.

A contract may simply include:

- An agreed-upon boundary
- Outlining the consequence if the boundary is broken
- Period of time that this contract will remain in place

- Signatures from both parties

My dad had several "contracts" with me as a teenager. They were not only about screens; he used them for anything in which I needed to learn responsibility. I still have a stack of those contracts in my keepsake bin. My dad almost always let me determine the consequence for violating a boundary, and the funny thing he gloats about to this day is that I always chose something more dire than he would have chosen. Nonetheless, he was teaching me responsibility and how to set boundaries for myself.

As a parent, you have opportunities to create those same types of contracts with your child regarding screen time. You can provide them with a new phone or tablet (or even access to the family TV), but in exchange, they need to agree to a certain level of responsibility.

You can create contracts concerning the types of content they are allowed to consume, which apps are accessed, which games are played, or the amount of time spent on a device. Once you agree upon these things, be sure to state when the contract will be revisited, revised, or renewed. Then help your child meet the expectations.

For example, if you agree how much time will be spent on a device, set an alarm with a five-minute warning so your child knows he needs to start saving his progress and shutting things down before the final alarm. Of course, many kids will test this boundary to see if the agreement is viable, so be prepared for conflict. Whether it's a game, a show, or an online chat, your kids will want to continue engaging with their screens beyond the time limit. You'll both need to know what to expect if those boundaries are broken.

The Bible has a lot to say about moderation. The idea of setting a limit is learning (or teaching a child) to live within healthy limits. If we are honest, this is a life skill that goes far beyond screens. 1 John 2:15–17 says, "Do not love the world or the things in the world." If we feast our eyes on the things of this world through our digital platforms, we will gain an appetite for things of this world that are not lasting or godly. Philippians 4:4 tells us to "let our moderation be known to all men"—meaning that we are not gluttons for anything, yet strive to take all things (even good things) in moderation.

Again, this is not just about contracts; it's an opportunity to add discipleship into every action we take with screens in our lives.

What Consequences Should You Set for Kids When They Break Rules?

When kids use their devices longer than they're allowed, or try to access their devices or unapproved content behind your back, you'll need to be ready with appropriate consequences for them. Perhaps the simplest (and often the most effective) consequence in this context is to take away their screen-time privilege, at least at home. If they cannot prove to be responsible with something, you take it away from them until they can change their behavior enough for you to let them try again. This is true with knives, money, cars, medicine, baseball bats, matches ... and digital devices.

Taking screens away tends to be an easy matter when you're raising younger children, but your older kids may have a school-issued laptop they need to use to do their homework. In these cases, you may require them to work at the dining room table instead of in their rooms so you can make sure they're only using it for schoolwork and not entertainment. It may also mean you have to have a conversation with the school's IT department to help you limit that device to certain school-related programs and timeframes.

Of course, you can apply any of your usual consequences, like grounding your kids, denying a play date, or curtailing social engagement—but removing their access to technology speaks to the specific boundary they violated. Also, many kids would rather play on their device than go outside, so grounding them might not be effective; it will only exacerbate the issue further and keep them from engaging in the type of behavior you want them to replace their screen time with anyway. You want them to abide by your tech rules because you expect them to be good digital citizens and respectful kids. When they choose not to honor your rules because their screens seem more important to them at the moment, remove those screens. Once your children know you're serious about pulling the plug on their technology access, they'll quickly step back in line.

As mad or frustrated as you may be, don't view violations as time to slap on a consequence. When our kids break a rule, it gives us an opportunity to connect with them. Conversation is an important element of discipleship and learning from mistakes. We want them to understand the why behind the rules. We want them to grow in their personal decision-making process and make choices from a place of wisdom, not just act out of fear of consequences. To mete out consequence without conversation will exasperate our kids (which Ephesians 6:4 warns us not to do). Our conversations must also be devoid of sarcasm or belittling—*What were you thinking? Have you lost your mind?* —and full of clarity and biblical instruction.

Turn off Devices an Hour Before Bedtime

As I previously mentioned, screen time can interrupt our sleep patterns. Watching television or playing video games stimulates the brain, making it hard for us to sleep. By turning off electronics before bedtime, you can encourage a calmer, more thoughtful, and mindful end to the day. That can be a time for engaging in quiet activities like reading, meditation, or prayer.

Kids' brains and bodies are still developing, and they require a good night's sleep each night. By setting aside this final hour of the day for calming activities, you can help them develop good habits that stretch beyond childhood. (Hey, it may be a good idea for you as an adult to avoid screen time an hour before bed, too. Just thought I'd sneak that in there.)

You can also create other boundaries. For instance, you may prefer to allow your elementary- and middle school-age kids to only use the internet on a community computer you keep in your family room or only where you can supervise their activities. If your older kids have phones, set some clear rules so they know they can't bring them to the dinner table or out to restaurants. These boundaries can help you raise well-adjusted children who understand that there are positive and negative ways to use technology.

More than anything else, children need healthy boundaries to help them develop the discipline and awareness it takes to thrive as an adult. With good discipleship and intentional dialogue, what they learn about boundaries around their screen time will better equip them to set healthy boundaries with work, relationships, and other essential aspects of adulthood.

CORE PRINCIPLE #7

IF YOU TEACH YOUR KIDS TO USE THEIR SCREENS IN MODERATION WHEN THEY ARE YOUNG, IT'S LIKELY THEY WILL CARRY THIS LIFE SKILL INTO ADULTHOOD.

CHAPTER 7

HELPING YOUR CHILD DEVELOP HEALTHY SCREEN HABITS

START WITH SCRIPTURE

"All things are lawful for me," but not all things are helpful. "All things are lawful for me," but I will not be dominated by anything. — 1 Corinthians 6:12

CORE PRINCIPLE #7

If you teach your kids to use their screens in moderation when they are young, it's likely they will carry this life skill into adulthood.

One night I was sitting in the corner chair in our family room, doing some things on my phone. I looked up from my screen to see that every single person in my family was also sitting there using a device. A few of the kids were watching one show on the TV, a few others had our old iPads out, my wife was on her phone, and one kid was on a laptop. Now, that may not seem like an odd picture to you—*if you have teens*. But all of my kids were under the age of eleven. Even our two-year-old was sitting in the glow of a screen. We were "together," but we were not truly together. We each had escaped to our own part of the cyberverse.

That night I said, "That's it! We are limiting screen time around here." I knew we needed to get healthier habits—all of us. I printed out coupons for screen time, something that looked like monopoly money, that I would use for them to "buy" time with a device. I peeled my daughters off their devices, and asked them to cut them out.

In my house, we now have two types of screen-time currency: individual screen time (for use on a laptop, tablet, or phone) and family screen time, which is used for the TV (someone else can watch with you, at no expense to them). The latter type of coupon is to promote teamwork and get the kids to make wise choices together.

There are various ways to go about this; I know my method was not perfect because we adapted it along the way. I gave the kids coupons based on their age and/or level of maturity. Here is what each child received:

The Coupons:

- **Individual Screen Time: The value of the coupons were in ten-minute denominations.** *I could have created various "lengths" of denominations (ten minutes, twenty minutes, etc.), but I thought I would keep it simple by keeping all the coupons small. This meant the older kids with larger allowances received more coupons.*

- **Family Screen Time: These coupons were good for any length** *(within reason) of a show that would be watched on the family TV, such as a movie, the Olympics, a TV show, or a sporting event. Other children could watch a show with someone who cashed in their family screen time coupon without getting a deduction from their bank. It just meant they might have to be the one to pony up next time they wanted to watch a show.*

The Allowances:

- **Chandler (eleven years old):** forty minutes per day (twenty-eight ten-minute coupons per week), two family coupons per week

- **Gracie (nine years old):** forty minutes per day (twenty-eight ten-minute coupons per week), one family coupon per week

- **Carolina (seven years old)**: thirty minutes a day (twenty-one ten-minute coupons per week), one family coupon per week

- **Daisy (five years old):** twenty minutes a day (fourteen ten-minute coupons per week)

- **Charlie (three years old):** twenty minutes a day (fourteen ten-minute coupons per week)
- **Patten (two months old):** No screen time needed, but his favorite channel is watching mom's ever move

You can earn more screen time by:

- *Reading a book*
- *Doing math problems*
- *Playing or creating something quietly for a designated period of time (for non-reading younger kids)*
- *Trading with a sibling (requires parental approval)*
- *At parent's discretion as a reward*

You can lose screen time by:

If we find that our kids are watching a disapproved show or using an app we do not allow, they will lose FOUR times the amount of the time they spent watching or engaging in that show or app. Parents also reserve the right to take away any number of coupons at any time for any reason.

Now you may be wondering, "Did that coupon thing actually work? Did they use them all in one sitting or spread them out over the week?" The answer to all those questions is "yes." Every one of our kids is different, and some kids ran out of their allotted screen time in the first three days. Others made it to the end of the week and had leftovers, so I started giving monetary rewards for those who had coupons left at the end of the week. On the other hand, if they ran out before the week's end, they had to read a good book or do a chore to earn more screen time.

For the most part, when the kids ran out, they just accepted it as a reality and found a better way to spend their free time for the rest of the week.

You may find that my allowances were too limiting or different from your conviction or the maturity of your child. That's fine because again, these are my children. I encourage you to make a healthy decision that's right for yours and help them learn limits.

Remember, not all technology is bad. It is the unbridled use of screens that we want to avoid. As you consider creating a healthier relationship with screens for your family, be realistic and keep the potential benefits of technology in mind. You will also want to factor in how much time your kids look at screens during their school day. This may mean you don't want your older kids interacting with a screen at home for two more hours in the afternoon or evening, or something comparable.

Nevertheless, screens aren't simply meant for entertainment. They're also a means for connecting with friends—and friendships become increasingly important as your older kids become teens. They help transition from being kids to being more independent and able to confidently interact with their peers. That's where being realistic helps. There's a lot to consider when we establish our ground rules regarding technology.

Let's explore some strategies to reduce screen time that may work for your household.

First, Communicate Your Expectations:

Let your kids know you are mindful of the amount of time they spend on screens, and you expect them to be mindful as well. You may feel inclined to explain why this is important, referring to the health benefits of reduced screen time and so forth, but you're not obligated to entertain a discussion that leads to debate. This is your household, and while it's helpful to be flexible and to listen, the decision about how to raise your kids is ultimately yours and your partner's. I am sure you've made it clear that your children will not eat only Fruit Loops and Fig Newtons; in the same way, explain why a balanced diet of digital consumption is important to you and your family. Avoid simplistic "because I said so" explanations and give them the "why" behind your rules. Tell them why this is for their benefit and that you are setting expectations because you love them.

Second, Set Aside Times to Unplug:

We've talked about the importance of unplugging from technology an hour before bedtime, but that's not the only time of the day you can set aside for screen reduction. When kids return from school, they may need their technology to do homework, so that may not be the best time to unplug. However, you'll find spots in your daily routine that are ideal for disconnecting from screens. Consider encouraging your children to get involved in fun activities outside the home. This will help them develop other interests that have nothing to do with screens.

The idea of "sabbath"—taking a day of rest—is important to us (but spoiler alert: we don't do this perfectly). If you were to come into our home most Friday evenings, you would find our family gathered around the table for a "Shabbat" meal. It isn't anything fancy, sometimes even leftovers. Our process includes the lighting of two candles that stand for "Remember" and "Keep" after the commands in Genesis to "Remember the sabbath" and "Keep it holy." Our kids even recite these words in Hebrew—*shamor* and *zakhor*. We say a prayer of blessing over the bread and grape juice, and I speak a blessing over each child. This begins our "day of rest."

Truth be told, we still do chores on our Sabbath; I often still have a sermon to finish, and life has other demands. But for the most part, we try to have a day of no-to-low technology usage, and I find that to be one of the most refreshing days of my week. A day of turning off devices, praying together, laughing, and eating together can be a reset from screens every family could use.

Third, Remove Technology from Bedrooms:

If your kids have a game console and TV in their bedroom, I strongly suggest you think about moving that device to a common space. These are temptations that will distract your child from other activities they might enjoy in their rooms, like reading or drawing. Of course, your teens may have their own laptops and smartphones, so taking these items away isn't going to make them savvy tech users.

A friend of mine just told me about an incident with her fifteen-year-old son who knows that phones are not allowed in the bedroom. She walked into his room and had a sense that he had broken that rule—call it mother's intuition or the Holy Spirit's prompting. She asked, "Is your phone in here?" to which he confidently replied, "No." No less than a second later, his pillow started to buzz and a slight glow emitted from the sheets. Let's just say that his sin found him out. So he lost his phone for a few days for lying and breaking the rules, but my friend told me that it hasn't been a problem since.

What will make our kids mindful of their tech usage? How can they connect with you and better understand your expectations regarding the healthy use of these devices? Of course you will need to check in and make sure they're on the right path, but remember that your sixteen- and seventeen-year-olds will be heading to college soon or searching for their first adult job. They need to know how to make their own smart choices. The older your child gets, the more their rules need to lighten and their responsibilities need to increase. Your goal is to help them make wise decisions on their own by the time they fly free.

Fourth, Protect Your Family Time:

You can reduce screen time for everyone in your family by having dinner together and setting aside other time to spend together. Each week, mark the calendar with things like:

- Friday evening is pizza and game night.
- Saturday afternoon or evening is for going on a family bike

ride, going roller skating, or visiting relatives.

- Sunday is for attending church and enjoying a family cookout afterward.
- Reserve an evening each week for teens and older kids to prepare dinner or help with meal preparation.
- Set aside time when everyone helps with outdoor chores.

Once you start brainstorming for ideas, you'll find loads of opportunities for cutting back on everyone's screen time.

Finally, Seek What Feeds Your Souls:

Not all screen time is created equal. Some shows and apps are spiritually beneficial, meaning the creators used technology to advance the message of the Gospel or biblical knowledge through screens. My kids have used The Bible for Kids app created by YouVersion for years. It reads Bible stories to them, has interactive elements on every screen, and even keeps track of the stories (or levels) they already completed. Other platforms, like Right Now Media, are full of Bible-based videos that keep my kids entertained for hours.

There are times I will allow "free screen time" for our kids (meaning that they don't have to use a Screen Time coupon) for spiritually nutritious content. They rarely complain when I tell them they can have time on a device as long as it's for one of the spiritually nurturing apps. If I'm honest, I even get pulled in by some of these apps and shows. They are fun, educational, and have a positive impact on the mind, body, and soul. You will never go wrong feeding your child's soul with the truths of Scripture.

CORE PRINCIPLE #8

EVERY MOMENT WE USE A SCREEN IS AN OPPORTUNITY TO BRING GLORY TO GOD.

CHAPTER 8

THE CHIEF END OF RAISING SCREEN TIME-SAVVY KIDS

START WITH SCRIPTURE

"So, whether you eat or drink, or whatever you do, do all to the glory of God." — 1 Corinthians 10:31

CORE PRINCIPLES #8

Every moment we use a screen is an opportunity to bring glory to God.

Many parenting books trumpet that the end-all, be-all purpose of parenting is *to ensure that our children are healthy and safe and prepared to make positive contributions to the world as adults.*

At first glance, that sounds noble, even admirable. What parent wouldn't be proud of raising great kids who have solid self-esteem and can affect their world for the better? Likely, you've encountered more than a few posts, podcast interviews, even sermons stating our job is to make sure we're sending great kids out into the world.

But what if I told you that the role of a parent is to glorify God more than it is to raise good kids?

We may argue, "Yeah, but raising good kids who are ready for a positive impact will glorify God." While that may be true, the target is essential, not incidental. I don't just wake up in the morning to ensure that I am providing my child with the food morsels and character morals that will sustain him. My mission is to glorify God and help my kids do the same.

Deuteronomy says that we are to talk about the things of God with our kids "as we walk along the road, as we lie down and get up" (Deuteronomy 6:4–7). Or, to put it in modern language, we speak about God as we drive in our SUVs, as we throw the football around together, read bedtime stories, or share our morning cereal.

As followers of Jesus, the ultimate responsibility of bringing God glory is stitched into the fabric of our faith. Being good simply for the sake of being seen as "good" is just image management. Even with the best intentions, changing our actions is only temporary and unsustainable because we are broken, imperfect humans. More importantly, perfectionism takes the spotlight off of giving God glory for how we engage with the world and tries to provide us with recognition for our behavior.

So, how does shifting the perspective from raising good kids to glorifying God align with the Gospel? It's reflected in how our souls turn from our young faith into becoming mature, engaged followers of Jesus. Parenting screen-time kids is about far more than what's on our screens; it's about seeing the chief end of our parenting efforts as an opportunity to glorify our Father in Heaven.

Soul Cravings and Maturing Appetites of Faith

The Apostle Peter wrote about the differences between baby food and adult food (1 Peter 2:2). When Molly, and I welcomed our sixth baby, Patten, I was still amazed to see that from his first moments with us, Patten instantly knew Mom's milk was what he needed.

As each of our kids started growing and maturing, their appetites changed—and so did their eating habits. They didn't want (or need) formula or milk anymore. No, my kids transitioned to grown-up food quickly. (Who doesn't love pizza night!) That shift was part of the natural maturation process. I didn't have to train my kids to go after real food; they started reaching for it naturally on their own as they grew.

Our souls crave the same type of development as our first seeds of faith blossom and we mature into committed, devoted followers of the ways and teachings of Jesus. Anyone who comes to Jesus has a faith that is new and needs tender, loving care. This is especially true for children. They need simple, foundational truths about who they are (children of God), who God is (their loving Heavenly Father), what Jesus did for us (died in our place to bring forgiveness and salvation for our souls), and who they can be (incredible followers of Jesus who can share His message with a broken, dark world).

Our parenting perspective always needs to keep the long-term picture in mind. The topic may be a screen today, but what's the more important lesson? How does this conversation about what's on their screens or how they're spending their time ultimately tie into what they believe about God and the Gospel?

Kids grow—times change. Technology is always going to be different, with greater appeal and more complexity than it held yesterday.

Our kids' souls grow and change as well. They understand different ideas and concepts about life, faith, relationships, and even the world as they mature. Growing older is inevitable, but maturing in our faith is a choice. Our parenting approach needs to develop in tandem with our kids' understanding of life through the lens of Scripture.

Turning Screen Savviness into Glorifying Moments

I fully recognize it can be hard to handle how screen time connects to giving glory to God, especially when trying to explain it to a child. That's why I've identified six God-glorifying benefits to teaching our kids how to be screen time-savvy:

1. **It shows our kids that good character stems from godly choices.**

How we choose to interact with screens in our lives tells the world what we believe is more important to us. A child who is ignoring you and refusing to turn off their screen is showing that their screen matters more to them at that moment than you do. Similarly, staying glued to your screen during family time also tells your child your screen matters more to you than he or she does at that moment.

2. Develop a pattern of resisting temptation.

With pornography, toxic relationship habits, and other destructive media never more than just a few taps away, screens will always present an opportunity to sin. The Apostle Peter's words remind us that we have a real enemy named Satan who is waiting for us to be vulnerable, like a lion waiting for its prey to be caught unaware (1 Peter 5). Being screen savvy means your child is aware that moments of temptation are always ahead of him. The Bible encourages us to deal with these moments with God's help. Hebrews 4:15 tells us that Jesus understands and "is able to empathize with our weaknesses, but we have one who has been tempted in every way, just as we are—yet he did not sin." His model is ours to emulate. God promises us a "way out" and provides us with the Holy Spirit's power to avoid falling for temptation and sin (1 Corinthians 10:13).

3. Take care of your mind and body.

Screen addiction is a real danger that many families are just now starting to address. The misuse of screens and technology is a household crisis that we must talk about as parents. It could save the life of someone you love, so our next chapter is dedicated entirely to navigating the mental and physical health issues associated with screen usage.

4. Take care of your emotions.

Who do I look to for fulfillment in my life? It's a question even many adults still struggle to answer positively. We can feel all sorts of emotions while reading a Twitter thread, watching a show, participating in a Zoom call, or even reading someone's pages-long response to a Facebook comment. What kinds of emotions are popping up with each type of screen you use? Being screen-savvy means we know how to keep our emotions in check while using our devices.

5. Teach your kids how to gain and maintain meaningful, engaging relationships.

This may not come as a shock to you, but social media isn't a real place. What is real are the people on the other side of the screens: in the DMs, in the comments thread, in the connection requests. Social media is an arena where kids can learn how to build meaningful, safe relationships with people who can stick with them for years to come.

6. Glorify God with the small decisions of obedience.

The Apostle Paul set the scene for the church in Corinth when he wrote in 1 Corinthians 10:31: "So, whether you eat or drink, or whatever you do, do all to the glory of God." No matter the situation, no matter how insignificant it may seem, every moment is a chance to show the world what God means to us. Our actions, words, and even thoughts can help us show up differently to the world as people being changed by our Savior, Jesus Christ.

Raising great adults means our kids understand and know how to live their lives for the glory of God well before they step out into the world. And as we both know, the world around us is filled with screens that carry the power to either give glory to God or deflect credit away from Him.

SCREEN ADDICTION IS A SERIOUS, CLINICALLY DIAGNOSABLE CONDITION THAT CAN HAVE DEVASTATING EFFECTS IF NOT ADDRESSED EARLY, INTENTIONALLY, AND BIBLICALLY.

CHAPTER 9

WHAT SHOULD YOU DO IF YOUR CHILD HAS AN ADDICTION
TO SCREENS AND REFUSES HELP?

START WITH SCRIPTURE

"For the grace of God has appeared, bringing salvation for all people, training us to renounce ungodliness and worldly passions, and to live self-controlled, upright, and godly lives in the present age..." — Titus 2:11-12

CORE PRINCIPLE #9

Screen addiction is a serious, clinically diagnosable condition that can have devastating effects if not addressed early, intentionally, and biblically.

I remember the first time I heard someone tell me, "Josh, I'm addicted to my phone." It seemed silly at the time. And then (to date myself), friends started referring to their Blackberry phones as their "Crackberries." Fast forward a few years to when app-based touchscreen devices entered the market and there we were, thumbing away at the newest dazzles on our digitals.

I'll confess I've struggled with being addicted to my phone—not in a diagnosable way, by the grace of God, but definitely in a way that means I give it far more attention than it needs or deserves.

This chapter stretches far beyond the "I spend too much time on my phone" realm that most of us occupy into what constitutes an actual, diagnosable addiction. The grim reality is that this is a real epidemic that is causing mental, emotional, spiritual, and in many cases permanent physical harm to children and teens.

All forms of addiction are dangerous to our well-being. They are governed by powerful feelings of compulsion that drive us to perform certain actions even though we are aware of their negative consequences. Children who develop screen addictions may not be aware that their technology use is actually harming them, so t's up to us as parents to help our children manage this problem and in time, overcome it.

Let's first come at this spiritually. The Apostle Paul wrote, "All things are lawful for me, 'but not all things are helpful. 'All things are lawful for me,' but I will not be enslaved by anything" (1 Corinthians 6:12). Addiction, by nature, is *disordered worship*—we are worshipping the created instead of the Creator. While self-control is a character issue to address with addiction, deeper still is the issue of worship and to whom or what we give our attention.

If we teach our kids to worship well, they can deal with their compulsion to obsess over technology correctly. Psalm 119:37 (NLT) says "Turn my eyes away from worthless things, and give me life through your word." In order to turn our eyes (or our kids' eyes) from the enthralling things of this world, we must help them develop an attitude of worship for God above all things.

It can be heart-wrenching to watch our children become veritable slaves to their screens, seemingly unable to drag themselves away. Screen dependency is increasingly viewed as a disorder that requires some degree of intervention to manage. According to Neurohealth Associates there are various kinds of screen and tech dependency that include:

- Internet gaming disorder
- Internet addiction
- Compulsive internet use
- Video game addiction
- Social media addiction, and more

The term "addiction" is increasingly used to describe the problematic behaviors kids exhibit in association with their screens, the internet, and technology. While these are merely man-made labels for an underlying spiritual condition, it does highlight the severity of the addiction.

What Are the Signs of Screen Addiction?

There are several concerning signs and symptoms parents need keep an eye out for. It's not uncommon for young kids to throw tantrums when they're suddenly told to stop playing their game or to put their device down, but that's not necessarily any more problematic than a child who won't leave the park or stop playing with a toy when instructed to do so. Signs and symptoms of a screen addiction, however, can include:

- Experiencing withdrawal when they are away from their devices (such as mood disturbances like irritability and depression)
- Lying about their screen use
- Losing interest in activities they once enjoyed
- Losing interest in seeing friends in person
- Continuing to use technology in spite of its negative consequences in the home or at school

Of course, addiction was not unknown to the ancients; the Bible refers many times to addictive types of behaviors, such as when Proverbs 25:28 tells us: "A man without self-control is like a city broken into and left without walls."

Helping Your Child Manage Screen Dependence

Parents need to remain present and vigilant in the management of this problem. Children and teens whose brains and bodies are still developing are vulnerable. We want to aid their growth and understanding, not hinder it. A screen addiction can affect their moods as well as their physical health. If you feel your child is obsessed with using screens and exhibiting worsening behaviors, you may be tempted to pull the plug on all technology—but remember that a short-term fix is powerless without a long-term strategy.

In extreme cases, it may be necessary to talk with your healthcare provider to address what the bible calls "Outer man" issues (2 Corinthians 4:16). I encourage you to get help from a pastor or biblical counselor who can also address the issues of the heart, as well as the external factors of behavior. In short, it can be managed, but you must be intentional.

Kids who develop a dependency upon screens often are unconcerned about it, at least in so much that they don't want to change. The truth is, they like playing videogames, browsing the internet, and connecting with people online. Unfortunately, they don't know how to use the off switch or why they should. Kids often don't have a complete awareness of what they're missing out on or what their tech addiction may be doing to their physical and mental health. However, parents do—or they certainly need to develop that awareness.

As I mentioned in a previous chapter, if you have a young child who is preoccupied with screens, you can gradually diminish that use each week. Consider the time they spend on their devices and gradually reduce that time until you achieve a manageable level. Once you do, be sure to maintain it with strict routines regarding homework time, reading time, bedtime, and so forth. Establishing a new and healthy routine provides your child with helpful structure.

Older kids who have a screen addiction can be more challenging—and if that's the case, it's important to seek help. A qualified biblical counselor or pastor can help your child understand what they're experiencing borders on a disorder and that they must, with the family's help, develop strategies for dealing with it.

There are two ways to handle a screen addiction—or any addiction, for that matter. First, just cut it off—"cold turkey." This can be very difficult and requires a high level of "staying power" for the parent. But it cannot come without support, teaching, love, and prayer for the child as he gets used to this drastic change.

The second option is to reduce the child's dependence on technology until their usage falls into a "normal" range. As we touched on earlier, some strategies that may be helpful include:

- Setting up media-free zones in the home, including bedrooms
- Designating no-media times or alternatively, setting media times
- Engaging in other activities
- Getting a part-time job (for kids age fifteen and older)
- Doing a set number of chores each day
- Not using technology until homework is completed

At the end of the day, what will change your child's thinking, motives, and behavior the most is a relationship with Jesus Christ. We cannot expect the work of the Holy Spirit and the fruits of the Spirit (like self-control) to be present until they know Him. Perhaps we can spend more time showing our child who Christ is and how He longs to help us in our weaknesses, including our own unhealthy longings and desires for that which Satan uses to "kill, steal and destroy" our lives (see John 10:10). Screens literally kill neural connections, steal our time, and destroy our relationships.

Once a person knows Jesus as his Lord and Savior, we are told to "take off" the ungodly actions and "put on" righteous ones (Ephesians 4:22–24). In the case of addictive tendencies, we can replace our device-dependent behaviors with:

- Worshiping God: our hearts are made more alive through worshiping our Lord.
- Creating something: we were made to create.
- Time in nature: learning to wonder at and be awed by God's creation.
- Reading the Bible reading: consuming God's living Word feeds us spiritually and instructs us with wisdom.

I will spend a few more minutes speaking about restricting and cutting back screen usage, but before I do, let's not miss this: all addictions are best handled by replacing them with something greater. It is best for us to relace our addictions with a love for God and desire what He desires over our own fleshly compulsions. Just as when teaching our kids about healthy eating, we don't just want to tell them what they can't have—we want to introduce them to good, nourishing foods so they crave those instead of junk. There are many good things God wants us to experience in our lives apart from technology; we don't want to miss these things because we were too busy staring at screen.

Your first goal as a parent should be to lead your children to know Christ. With His help in their lives, they will be able to take their eyes off what is below and fix them on what is above (Colossians 3:2).

Weniger Aber Besser (Less but Better)

Dieter Rams was a famous German designer who prized his work on the simple yet profound. He is credited with hundreds of iconic products—ranging from the Oral-B toothbrush and portable radios to coffeemakers and calculators, shelving systems and compact televisions. When asked about his approach to creating, he used the German phrase, *"Weniger Aber Besser"* which means, "Less but better."

The idea of less but better is a fine design principle, but it can also apply to our (or our kids') use of screens. We should not just "limit" but *also* "replace" with something better. This is "putting off" and "putting on" as Paul talked about in Ephesians 4:22–24.

When you take the important steps to limit screen time and are mindful of what your child does with technology, you're going to enjoy some unmistakable benefits. As parents who have been out in the world, we know there is so much more out there to explore. When our kids do this, there will be a greater benefit in their development.

Benefit #1: Supports Physical Health

Sitting down for hours staring at a screen is NOT conducive to physical health. Obesity is a significant problem among children. By reducing screen time and encouraging outdoor play and exercise, you can ensure your child stays mindful of his fitness needs.

Benefit #2: Improves Social Connections

Kids need to develop social skills. Texting their friends isn't the pinnacle of social connection. We want our kids to have face-to-face, in-person experiences with their friends, relatives, and other people in the community so they can develop important skills related to communication and positive interactions with other humans.

Benefit #3: Supports Mental Health

Too much screen time can undermine a good mood. When you reduce screen time, you can encourage mood-enhancing pursuits like participating in a local youth group, connecting with nature, trying out a new sport, or exercising. The World Health Organization estimates that by 2030, a sedentary lifestyle will be a leading cause of depression for people over twelve years old, worldwide.[1] Help your child safeguard his mental health by regulating his use of technology and incorporating other activities into his daily life.

Benefit #4: The Chance to Learn New Things

When you reduce screen time, you actually "force" your kids to find other things to do—things they might actually grow to love. Many activities that can enrich your child's life, like reading, have a tough time competing with technology because nonscreen activities require more self-discipline and lack the immediate stimulation/reward process of technology. You can even the playing

1 Association between screen time and depression among US adults, August 16, 2017, https://www.ncbi.nlm.nih.gov/pmc/articles/PMC5574844/ accessed on November 25, 2021

field for these worthwhile pastimes by pulling the plug on your kids' devices each day at a certain time. They can spend that extra time learning a new skill like gardening, sewing, building a treehouse, baking, or learning a new language.

"An intelligent heart acquires knowledge, and the ear of the wise seeks knowledge." (Proverbs 18:15).

Help your kids understand that knowledge comes in different forms, and a screen cannot provide all the knowledge they'll need over the course of their lives. The activities they come to enjoy separately from screens can support a healthy lifestyle. The time they spend playing videogames and watching cartoons, while enjoyable, detracts from the time they can spend learning essential life skills. Remember, you're doing your children a tremendous service by limiting their screen time, no matter how much they may think otherwise.

CORE PRINCIPLE #10

SCREENS, LIKE MONEY OR TIME, ARE AMORAL IN NATURE. IT'S HOW WE USE THOSE DEVICES TO FULFILL THE GREATEST COMMANDMENT OF CHRIST THAT MATTERS MOST.

CHAPTER 10

THE ONLY TWO RULES YOU NEED

START WITH SCRIPTURE

"I have no greater joy than this, to hear my children are walking in the truth." — 3 John 1:4

CORE PRINCIPLE #10

Screens, like money or time, are amoral in nature. It's how we use those devices to fulfill the greatest commandment of Christ that matters most.

Molly and I were sitting at Ted's Montana Grill, eating bison burgers with our friends Ken and Laura. This pastor and his wife had raised five kids who were all walking with the Lord, and Molly and I had sought their advice on the seemingly overwhelming task of caring for the six little souls that God had entrusted to us.

I nearly choked on my onion ring when Ken said he only had two rules in his home. I already had dozens of rules for our kids, and we weren't even a quarter of the way through raising our first child. "You must be joking!" I said. He wasn't.

The Murphy house rules were simple— but profound:

1. Love Christ.
2. Love others.

Ken and Laura explained that every decision their children had to make must first pass through those filters, based on the greatest commandment outlined by Christ (see Matthew 22:35–40, Mark 12:28–34, and Luke 10:27).

While there may be needs for other "rules" or guidelines in this life, they all can come back to these two questions:

1. Does what I am about to do please Christ or bring me to love Him more?
2. Does what I am about to do show love toward others, more than loving myself?

Watching a video that is "junk food" for our soul doesn't help us love Christ. A broken curfew is loving oneself and not loving others (namely the wide-awake and waiting parent). Making fun of someone online (or watching a video of others doing so) doesn't love others. Lusting over what someone else has or looks like online does not help us love Christ or others.

Like anything else in our lives, tech use is an opportunity for discipleship, a chance to teach our kids how to love Jesus and be more like Him. More important than maintaining the proper rules or creating the right consequences for breaking them, we want to cultivate a love for Christ in our own lives and the lives of our kids.

So, the question becomes: what are you doing to encourage your child toward Christ? Where do you worship more—by the light of your phone or in the glory of His presence?

The greatest gift you can ever give your children is the invitation to know Jesus personally. We must:

- **Explain to our kids that God is perfect and holy; He is worthy of our greatest affection.** He desired an unhindered relationship with us, but He must punish our sin (1 John 1:5, Revelations 4:11, Romans 2:5–8).

- **Help our kids recognize that their sin stands in the way of that unhindered relationship.** Sin is not just something we do; it is part of our nature. From birth, we are alienated from God (Ephesians 2:1–3).

- **Show them the significance of Christ's death and resurrection to allow our forgiveness and give us access to God's power.** Our sinless Savior died in our place, bearing God's wrath for us. All who believe in Him will have an eternal relationship of joy with their Creator (John 1:1, 1 Timothy 2:5, Hebrews 7:26, Romans 3:21–26, 2 Corinthians 5:21, 1 Corinthians 15:20–22).

- **Lead them to respond by living a life of repentance, faith, and obedience to Christ.** We are promised that if we turn from our sin and trust in Christ, we will be saved eternally (Mark 1:15, Acts 20:21, Romans 10:9–10).

As parents, what God has asked of us is not something we can merely muscle through with determination and grit. We are to point our children to the things of God "as we walk along the road, as we lie down, and as we get up" (Deuteronomy 6:5–7). Our efforts must be coupled with God's divine power to call our kids to believe in Christ and follow Him. As we lead them to meet Jesus, we trust the result of salvation to God. Charles Spurgeon wrote in his book, Spiritual Parenting, "Gather the little ones around your knee and listen to their words, suggesting to them their needs, and reminding them of God's gracious promise." This is our greatest calling!

Loving Others More Than Ourselves

Our kids live in this world and are part of it. The trappings of the world will always compete for their attention. We must show our children what constitutes a good, healthy, others-focused, and Christ-centered lifestyle. They are looking to us to learn what a faithful Christian life should look like. When kids have a stable Christian home structure based on biblical principles, they stand on surer footing when faced with obstacles, challenges, or distractions. Stability and values arm them against chaos and disorder. Every parent who is a follower of Jesus understands the conflict between the things of the Spirit and the things of this world.

Thus far, we've stuck to discussing the problem at hand—the need to reduce or correct screen time—but technology is just one aspect of this modern world that may compete with our or our children's focus on faith. There are always distractions. We know them by many different names: screen addiction, underage drinking, reality television, celebrity crushes, teen romance, and many other labels. Many opportunities in our lives can detract us from leading the life we want—the life we know our faith encourages us to lead.

As parents, we want our kids to master these distractions and temptations. We can help them by providing a clear mindset regarding technology and every other distraction they may encounter. As they develop the discipline to live by loving Christ and loving others, they will reap a lifetime of godly decisions that please Christ.

Self-control is the key to effective screen-time management. Our goal as parents is to help our young children manage their use of technology in healthy ways. Then we can help our older children begin to control their own use of technology while remaining on the lookout for signs of problems so that we can guide them to safer shores. Remember to model the proper behavior regarding tech use for your children and stay consistent about following your own screen-time rules.

When we first moved into our current home, there was a *massive* grapevine in the backyard. The previous owner wanted to bring a piece of California to Colorado by allowing this vine to grow and take over the space. Much to my consternation, it was making the fence buckle under its weight, as well as taking over the nearby trees and our lawn. When I started calling other vine-dressers (while pretending to be one), they told me I needed to build a trellis for the vine. It needed some wood framework to be able to grow and attach itself to. If I gave it something to climb, it would remain attached to that and subsequently detach from everything else.

I found out the word "trellis" comes from the Latin word *regula*, which can also be translated "rule." Often the areas that seem to take over our lives are the most are unstructured and lacking discipline—or *regula*. Screen time can get away from us just as fast, if not faster, than that old grapevine in my backyard. In the same way that a vine needs to be lifted off the ground so it can bear fruit and enjoy protection from predators, so our lives must have the right "Trellis" for us to abide in Christ. Jesus uses the vine illustration in John 15:1–8 as a picture of the closeness we should have with our Heavenly Father. To aid our children in knowing Christ and being like Him, we need to be good at building and repairing trellises (rules) in their lives.

Creating the right trellis for my grapevine demanded that I cut it back i first. Perhaps the same thing needs to happen with your family's screen time? You may need to cut it back, then put the right guidance in place, and then allow it to return to a healthy amount.

It may be worth asking, "How does the speed of my family's life encourage a reliance on technology?" For instance, if Mom and Dad need to work or get things done and are turning screens into babysitters for the kids, does something else need to go? Are we too busy elsewhere for things like spending time and eating dinner together? What rhythms of sabbath need to be installed so the family can detox from technology and reconnect in relationships?

As you seek to apply the material we've covered in this book, here are some more questions to help you further evaluate what is missing, needs repair, or must be pruned in your life:

- How much time do you spend on your own screen in a given week? (Use your phone's screen time app to check.)

- How much time do your kids spend on screens in a week? (Let this be a "typical" week and track their exact time.)

- How often do you sit down together for a screen-free dinner?

- How much time every day do you spend with your child without screens?

- What are you doing to cultivate a love for the Lord in your home? How can you help your kids learn to worship?

- What are some reasons you turn to screens? Boredom? Loneliness? Escapism? Procrastination? How can you deal with those underlying issues without turning to a screen?

- Who can be a source of accountability for you in your own screen use?

- Think about the end of your life and what you hope your kids remember about your home. What do you need to do now to help create that legacy?

- What is your next step when it comes to how your family handles screen time?

You're Not Alone

If you're struggling with screen time in your home, it's likely that other families around you are, too. Talk to your Christian friends, school administrators, or church leaders about what you're facing. They may have helpful suggestions for you. Your pastor or youth group leader may also help you adopt helpful, practical strategies for dealing with technology use in your home.

No matter what your situation may be, always remember we have a loving Father in Heaven who understands what you're feeling. He's always here, ready to give you the wisdom and strength you need to lead your child well. Lean into His wisdom. Dive into Scripture. Trust that He will give you the exact insight you need to help your child have a healthy relationship with screens—both now and in the future.

THANK YOU

Thank you, Cassie Baker, for being a constant source of encouragement to keep writing. You are a dear friend, a fantastic sidekick, and a faithful partner in the Gospel.

Thank you, Mike Ruman, for being one of my most faithful friends, giving selflessly, and believing in me when I don't.

Thank you, Jon Cook, for carrying this project forward when I was too weak and distracted with Patten's sickness to keep going.

Thank you, Donna Cook, for combing every word to add what I miss and make this project better. You make the task of writing a joy.

Thank you, Catherine Fitzgerald, for challenging me to write better content by helping me think biblically and practically.

Thank you, Karla Dial, for jumping back in with me so quickly and being the perfect running partner for crossing every finish line.

Thank you, Mitch Bolton, for always creating inspiring covers, for your detail in design, and for the friendship we share. I praise God that He has preserved your life!

Thank you, Mike Salisbury, for being the exact coach I needed in the boxing ring corner when I was ready to tap out.

Thank you, Grace Chapel, for your endless trust, support, and encouragement to keep leading people to find and follow Jesus.

Thank you, Chandler, Gracie, Carolina, Daisy, Charlie, and Patten, for letting me use you as examples in my writing and preaching (I owe you ice cream!). God uses you to teach me daily. My most tremendous honor in life is to be called your "Dad."

Thank you, Molly My Love, for allowing me to do early mornings at the coffee shop and tend to outside projects for the sake of the Gospel. I couldn't ask for a better wife, friend, and counterpart. You make me a better man. I love you.

...For the glory of Christ Jesus, my Lord.